THE GREEN REBEL
ACTIVITY BOOK

Buster Books

Illustrated by
Berta Maluenda

Written by
Frances Evans and
Josephine Southon

Edited by Frances Evans

Designed by
Zoe Bradley

Cover designed by
John Bigwood

First published in Great Britain in 2021 by Buster Books, an imprint of
Michael O'Mara Books Limited, 9 Lion Yard, Tremadoc Road, London SW4 7NQ

W www.mombooks.com/buster   f Buster Books   🐦 @BusterBooks

Copyright © 2021 Buster Books

ISBN: 978-1-78055-711-3

1 3 5 7 9 10 8 6 4 2

This book was printed in January 2021 by Leo Paper Products Ltd,
Heshan Astros Printing Limited, Xuantan Temple Industrial Zone,
Gulao Town, Heshan City, Guangdong Province, China.

MIX
Paper from
responsible sources
FSC
www.fsc.org   FSC® C020056

HELLO, GREEN REBEL!

If you've picked up this *book*, the chances are you want to make a difference to the future of our planet. That's what *being a Green Rebel* is all about. The good news is that these pages contain everything you need to start a **green revolution** at home right now.

There are fun puzzles, brain games and activities to tackle that explore **eco topics**, such as plastic pollution, saving water and composting. Along the way, you'll discover **hands-on tips** you can use to help the planet. All the answers are at the back of the *book* if you get stuck.

Join Forces
The choices and actions that we make in our everyday lives really can change the future of the planet. Being a Green Rebel is about **working together** – with family, friends, people in your local community and campaigners across the globe – to make an important contribution to our **amazing world**.

RIVER CLEAN-UP

These volunteers are picking up rubbish in their local river to help wildlife thrive there.

Can you spot ten differences between the two scenes?

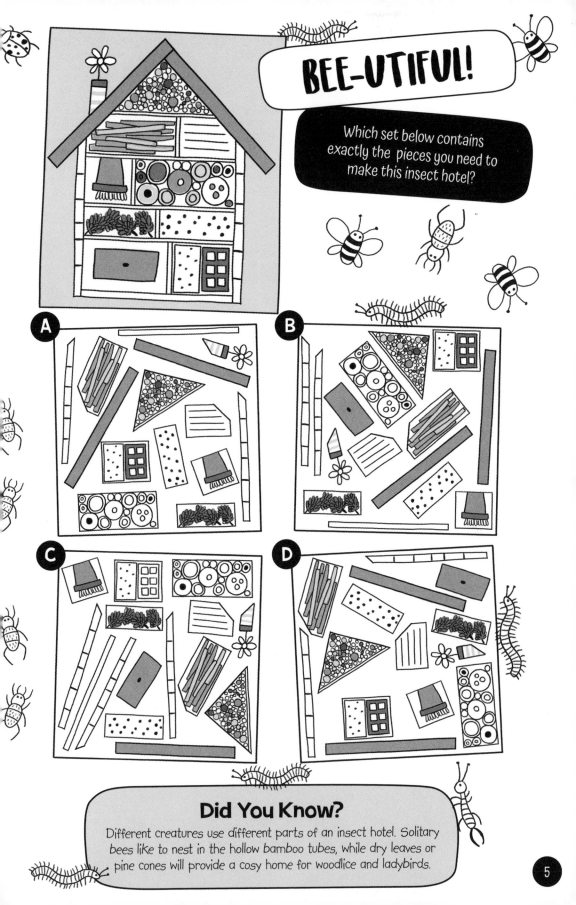

BEE-UTIFUL!

Which set below contains exactly the pieces you need to make this insect hotel?

A

B

C

D

Did You Know?
Different creatures use different parts of an insect hotel. Solitary bees like to nest in the hollow bamboo tubes, while dry leaves or pine cones will provide a cosy home for woodlice and ladybirds.

LOVE YOUR LEFTOVERS

Thinking up ways to use leftover ingredients in your fridge is a great way to cut down on the amount of waste that hits the food bin. You can freeze browning bananas for use in smoothies, for instance, or make some yummy potato cakes from leftover mash.

How many ideas for meals can you come up with, using some or all of the ingredients in this leftover list?

Leftover List

- 3 tomatoes
- A piece of cheese
- A slice of ham
- A bowl of pasta
- 2 eggs
- Some lettuce
- Half a pepper
- 2 slices of bread

PIPE PUZZLE

One way of reducing water waste in the garden is by collecting rainwater in barrels called 'butts'. This free, natural water can be used to water plants or wash your bike, rather than using water from the tap.

Can you work out which pipe leads to the water butt?

A B C D

BUTT

Top Tip
You can make your own water butt by reusing an old plastic bin and placing it under the guttering. An adult will need to drill a hole in the lid and in the top of the drainpipe, and add a tap at the base of the bin.

GO GREEN

This family have tried to make their house and garden as green as possible.

Can you spot ten eco-friendly things in the scene on the opposite page? List all the things you can spot in the space below and say why you think they are good for the environment.

Don't worry if you can't spot them all or aren't sure why they are eco-friendly – if you turn to the answer page, they are explained there in more detail.

POLLINATOR SUDOKU

Pollinators are animals that move pollen from the male part of one flower to the female part of another flower. By doing this, they help the plant to reproduce. Bees are well-known pollinators, but many other insects and animals are pollinators, too.

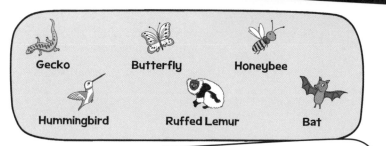

Gecko   Butterfly   Honeybee

Hummingbird   Ruffed Lemur   Bat

Example:

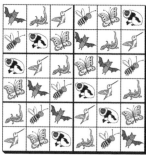

Can you complete this grid so that every row, column and 2x3 mini-grid contains all six of these pollinating creatures? Use the smaller example grid to see what you need to do.

POLLINATOR POWER

Study this scene of bee- and butterfly-friendly plants for one minute. Then turn the page and see how much you can remember about it.

Apple tree

Ivy

Chives

Lavender

Sedum

Rosemary

Dandelions

Strawberry

Crocus

QUESTIONS

1. What kind of tree was in the picture?

2. Can you write down all of the other pollinating plants you can remember from the scene?

3. What fruit was featured in the picture, and how many individual fruits did you count?

4. What object was lying on the grass?

5. How many bugs did you spot in the picture?

BOTTLE MATCH-UP

Match up the identical pairs of reusable water bottles. Which two don't have a twin?

DOLPHIN DILEMMA

Which stream should the river dolphin take to safely reach the shoal of tasty fish? Watch out for fishing nets, dams and dead ends.

A B C D

Did You Know?

The endangered Ganges river dolphin only lives in freshwater and its habitat is under threat from dams, pollution and over-fishing. Charities such as the World Wildlife Fund are working to encourage local communities to protect the species.

ORANGUTAN STATS

These incredible apes live in the forests of Indonesia and Malaysia, but their habitat is rapidly disappearing. Solve these number sequences to discover some key stats about them. Start with the number on the left and perform each sum in turn to get the final result.

A

26 − 8 ÷ 2 − 6 =
The number of orangutan species

B

5 × 4 + 28.5 × 2 =
The percentage of DNA that humans share with orangutans

C

104 ÷ 4 − 14 ÷ 6 =
The average arm span (in metres) of an adult male orangutan

D

16 × 3 + 52 ÷ 2 =
The average age of an orangutan in the wild

E

30 + 42 ÷ 4 − 11 =
The number of years that young orangutans stay with their mothers

QUICK FIX

Lucy's favourite mug has broken. Rather than throw it away, Lucy wants to repair it and use it to hold her paint brushes and pencils.

Can you work out which five pieces below fit together to make the mug on the left?

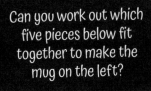

Top Tip

Before you throw something broken away, always ask yourself if it could be repaired or reused in some way. Finding a creative use for an old item can be fun and save you money, and it also means one less thing going to landfill (a rubbish dump).

RUNNING ON EMPTY

These four electric cars are running low on energy.

Which car is on a road that will lead it to the charging point?

Charging point

TURBINE JUMBLE

How many wind turbines can you count in the jumble below?

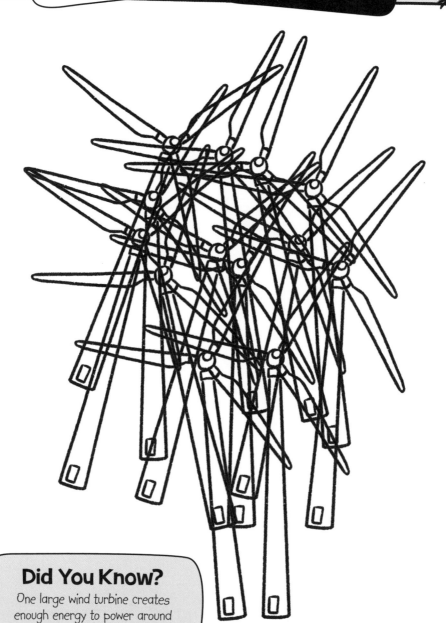

Did You Know?

One large wind turbine creates enough energy to power around 600 US homes for a whole year.

Can you help this caterpillar climb down the living wall by following the plants in the following sequence? You can move across, up and down but not diagonally.

START

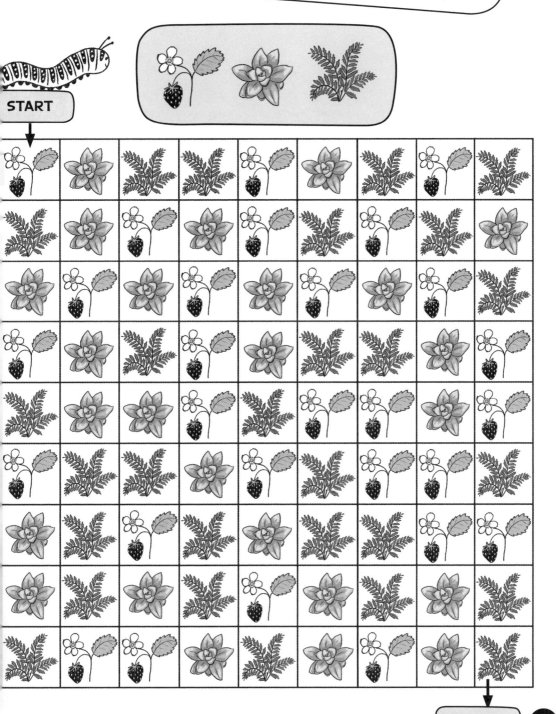

FINISH

CLIMATE MARCH

Add your own climate messages and designs to these banners.

PLASTIC PROBLEM

Can you spot four plastic bags floating among these jellyfish?

Did You Know?

Around 700 species of marine animals – including endangered ones – are known to have been affected by plastic pollution.

DIY NO-SEW BAG

Follow these simple steps to make your own eco-friendly tote bag from an old T-shirt.

You will need:

- An old T-shirt
- Scissors (always ask an adult before using them)
- A ruler
- Masking tape

Step 1:
Cut off the sleeves and neckline on the T-shirt as shown. Cut the sleeves off just past the seam line where the sleeves join the top. Cut the neckline in an oval shape rather than a round shape, so the arms of your bag are a good length.

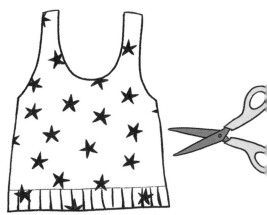

Step 2:
Your T-shirt should now look like this. Use a ruler to work out how deep you want your bag to be and mark this line with masking tape.

Step 3:
Make even cuts from the bottom of the shirt up to the line of masking tape to form a fringe. Cut both the front and back of the T-shirt at the same time to get even strips. Remember to cut the pieces at either end of the shirt in two.

Step 4:
Turn the T-shirt inside out and start tying the front and back pieces together.

Step 5:
Your bag is starting to take shape! It should now look like this. Notice that there are gaps between the ties.

No sewing required!

Step 6:
To close up these gaps, tie the strips on either side of each gap together.

Step 7:
Turn the bag right side out, and it is ready to hit the shops!

COMPOST CHAMPIONS

These compost bins are full of healthy compost, but which compost is the best?

Add up the points to find out. The bin with the highest score has the best compost.

 Grass clippings = 1 point

 Apple core = 2 points

Egg shell = 3 points

 Banana skin = 4 points

Shredded newspaper = 5 points

 Potato peel = 6 points

 Dead leaves = 7 points

A Total ....

B Total ....

C Total ....

GROW GREEN

Growing even a small amount of fruit and veg yourself can help the planet.

Can you find the following groups of home-grown vegetables in this busy veg patch?

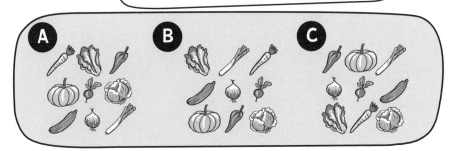

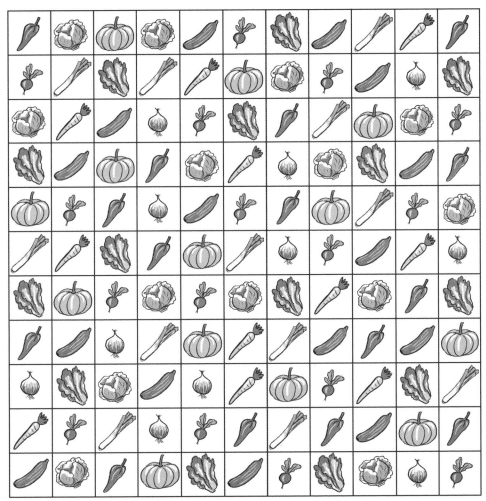

Top Tip

Even if you don't have a garden, you can still grow fruit and veg. Try planting lettuces or tomatoes in window boxes, or use an old egg box to grow a mini herb garden.

ECO HOME

Ezra and Laila's family have a weekly rota for household jobs. Read each person's to-do list below and work out who does which job on each day of the week.

Fill in each name on the chart on the opposite page. One name has been filled in to help you.

Mum's to-do list:

Cook a meat-free meal three days after Dad and Laila cook theirs.

Do a food shop the day before Ezra washes his bike.

Dad's to-do list:

Cook a meat-free meal on the first day of the week.

Do a clothes wash four days after Laila waters the plants.

Ezra's to-do list:

Empty the compost on the day that Laila sorts the recycling.

Water the plants on the day that Dad does a clothes wash.

Help Mum cook a meat-free meal.

Wash bike at the end of the weekend.

Laila's to-do list:

Water the plants on the second day of the week.

Sort the recycling on the next day.

Help Mum with a food shop.

Help Dad cook a meat-free meal.

	MONDAY	TUESDAY	WEDNESDAY	THURSDAY	FRIDAY	SATURDAY	SUNDAY
Water the plants		Laila					
Sort the recycling							
Empty the compost							
Cook a meat-free meal							
Do a food shop							
Do a clothes wash							
Clean the bike							

27

WONKY VEG WASTE

Wonky vegetables are veggies that used to be thrown away by shops for being too big, small or ugly. Which of these silhouettes matches this box of wonky veg exactly?

Top Tip
Wonky fruit and vegetables taste exactly the same as 'perfect' fruit and veg, and many supermarkets are now starting to relax their rules about stocking them. Support these schemes by encouraging your parents to buy 'wonky' groceries the next time they do a shop.

ECO ENERGY

These houses get their electricity from different forms of alternative energy. Follow the electricity wires to find out which house is powered by which form of energy.

Hydroelectricity

Solar power

Nuclear

Wind power

Did You Know?

Around 71% of the world's renewable energy comes from hydroelectric power. China produces the most hydroelectricity and is home to the world's largest hydroelectric dam – the Three Gorges Dam, which spans the Yangtze River.

ON YOUR BIKE!

Amira, Jess and Ryan ride their bikes to school. Their bikes are three different sizes and each one is a special eco model – one is called the 'Eco Warrior', one is called the 'Pedal Powerer' and one is called the 'Green Goer'.

Can you use the clues below to work out which bike is which and who owns it? Draw a line to match them up when you've solved it.

Amira

Jess

Ryan

- Ryan's bike is larger than Amira's bike.
- Amira's bike is not called the Green Goer.
- The bike called the Pedal Powerer is the smallest.
- Amira's bike is not the smallest.

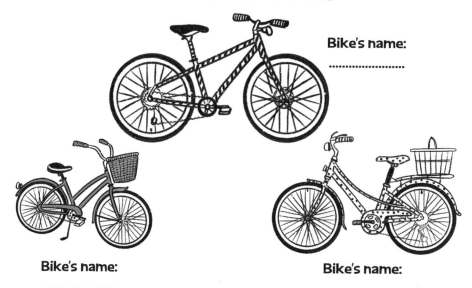

Bike's name:
....

Bike's name:
....

Bike's name:
....

SHOE MATCH-UP

Jay is going to donate his family's unused shoes to charity. But first he needs to match them into pairs.

Can you help him? Which shoes don't have partners?

Did You Know?

A study by the charity Oxfam found that every person in the UK has an average of seven pairs of unwanted shoes each.

SMALL ACTIONS, BIG CHANGE

Can you match the correct sentence halves together to learn some mind-blowing eco facts? One has been done for you to get you started.

The energy saved from recycling one glass bottle	saves between 15 and 17 mature trees.
Making aluminium from recycled materials	is dumped into the ocean.
Turning off the tap when you brush your teeth	will operate a 100-watt light bulb for four hours.
Preventing one tonne of paper waste	you can save 466 items of unnecessary plastic every year.
A ten-year-old TV left on standby	takes 95% less energy than using raw materials.
By carrying reusable cutlery or reusing your plastic cutlery	can save over 24 litres of water a day.
Every year, eight million tonnes of plastic waste	uses 12 watts per hour.

RECYCLING SUDOKU

Can you complete the grid so that every row, column and 2x3 mini-grid contains all six of the following materials that you can recycle? Use the smaller example grid to see what you need to do.

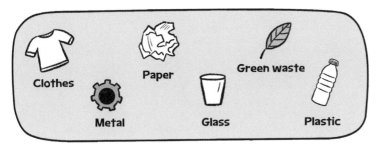

Clothes

Metal

Paper

Glass

Green waste

Plastic

Example:

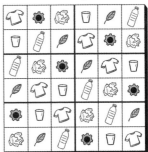

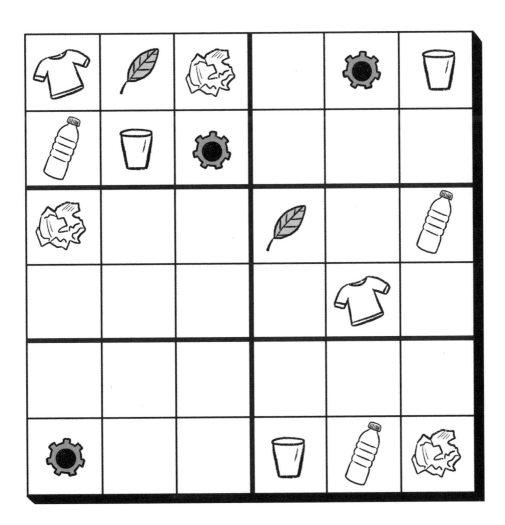

PLANT POWER

Luca is helping to plant young oak trees – called saplings – in his local nature reserve. It takes Luca 9 minutes to plant one sapling.

By counting the number of saplings, including the one Luca is holding, can you work out how long will it take him to plant all of the saplings in the picture?

TREE-RIFIC

Complete these maths sequences to discover some tremendous stats about trees. Start with the number at the top and perform each sum in turn to get the final result.

A

2

+ 4

x 9

− 4

x 100

=

The age of the oldest tree on the planet

B

14

+ 6

x 5

x 10

x 2

=

The number of species of birds, insects and other living things that can live in a single tree in the Amazon rainforest

C

8

x 6

+ 5

+ 10

÷ 3

=

The average amount of carbon dioxide in kilograms that a mature tree can absorb in a year

D

7

x 3

+ 4

x 5

− 18

=

The height in metres that a redwood tree can grow to

35

SMART THINKING

Can you work out how much energy each of the appliances along the bottom of the page uses? The total amount of each row and column is shown on smart metres on the right and bottom of the grid. One answer has been given already to help you.

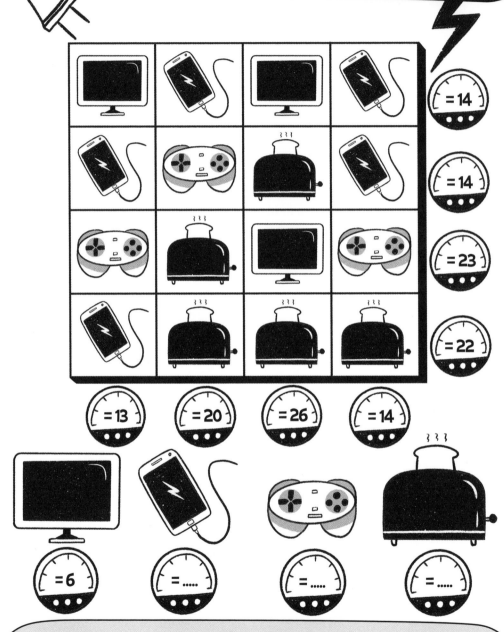

Top Tip

If you have a smart metre in your home, you can see how much your energy usage costs per day. Take a look at the metre before you play a video game, for instance, and see how much it has gone up by afterwards. By getting a sense of how much energy each appliance in your home needs, you can start to think about how you can reduce your energy use.

SPREAD THE WORD!

Is there a local environmental campaign you feel strongly about? Maybe you think more trees should be planted near your school or more could be done in your hometown to help people recycle. Write a letter to a politician or important figure, explaining your cause and what you think needs to be done.

One of the biggest threats facing wild sloths is the way their habitat has been broken up by roads. To help sloths cross roads safely, conservationists have put up rope bridges.

Can you work out which tree each sloth is heading to by following their route along the rope?

A LOAD OF RUBBISH

This pile of rubbish hasn't been sorted through properly.

Can you work out how many items need to go in the food waste bin, the paper and cardboard bin, and the glass, plastic and tin bin?

Paper and Cardboard

Glass, Plastic and Tins

Food Waste

LEOPARD TRAIL

With only 100 individuals left in the wild, Amur leopards are thought to be the rarest big cat in the world.

Can you help the Amur leopard reach her cubs by following the trail of pawprints in the order shown below? You can move across, up and down but not diagonally.

START

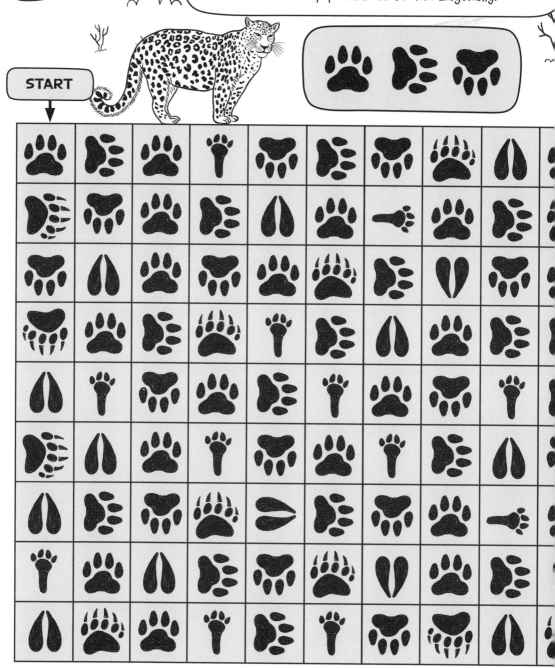

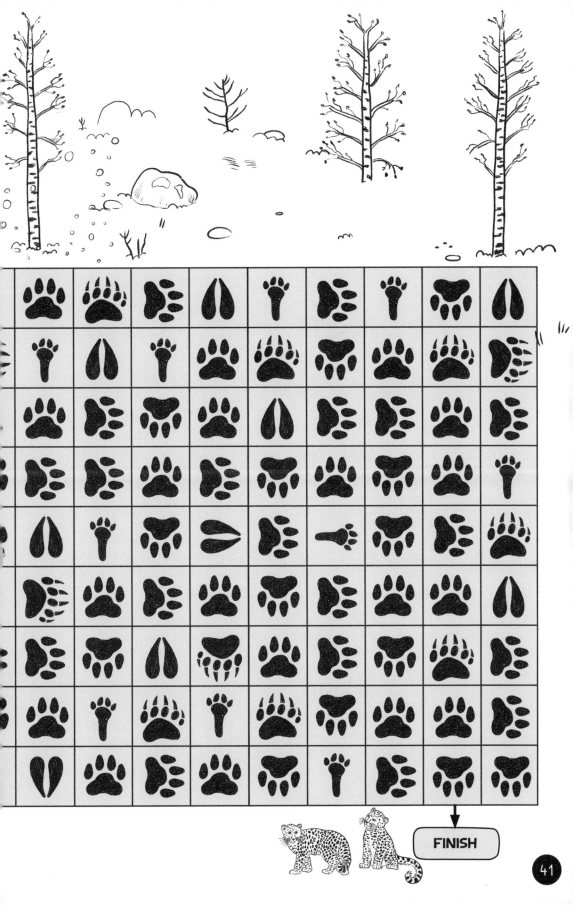

FINISH

41

THIS OLD THING

Finding new uses for old or worn out clothes is a great way to keep your stuff out of landfill.

How many creative ways can you think of to revamp or reuse an old T-shirt? Write down as many ideas as you can on the T-shirt below.

BLUE

RED

LUNCHBOX WARS

By totting up the plus and minus points, can you work out which of these lunchboxes has the most points and is therefore the most eco-friendly?

 Leftover pasta = 1 point

 A piece of fruit = 1 point

A portion of veg = 2 points

 Cling film or tin foil = −2 points

− points for:

+ points for:

 Metal cutlery = 2 points

 Reusable water bottle = 3 points

 Beeswax wrap = 4 points

 Single-use crisp packet = −1 point

 Plastic cutlery = −1 point

 Single-use bottle = −3 points

A Total ....

B Total ....

C Total ....

DIY HERB GARDEN

Follow these simple steps to transform an old plastic bottle into a herb garden.

You will need:

- 1-litre plastic water bottle (with sticker removed)
- Pen
- Scissors (ask an adult before using)
- String
- Ruler
- Potting soil
- Herb seeds (such as basil, chives, thyme and oregano)

Step 1:
Cut two pieces of string that are about the same length as your bottle.

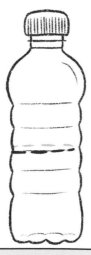

Step 2:
Measure halfway from the bottom of the bottle and make a mark with your pen. Ask an adult to cut all the way around the bottle at the mark.

Step 3:
Take the top half of the bottle and make four small holes around the neck, about I cm below the cap.

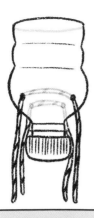

Step 4:

Thread one piece of string through two of the holes, and thread the other piece of string through the remaining two holes.

Step 5:

Fill the bottom of the bottle with water and place the top piece, cap end down, into the bottom half. The strings should be hanging into the water.

Step 6:

Fill half of the top bottle piece with potting soil. Then add approximately four seeds and add a little soil on top of them, pressing it down gently.

Step 7:

Place the bottle in a sunny spot and top up the water in the base whenever it looks low. The string will soak up the water into the soil, watering the seeds as they grow.

HOW ECO-FRIENDLY ARE YOU?

Answer the questions below about your day-to-day activities. At the end, add up how many As, Bs, Cs and Ds you circled, and turn to the answer page to find out how eco-friendly you are.

1. How would you best describe your diet?

a) Vegetarian/vegan
b) I eat fish but not red meat
c) Meat in some meals
d) Meat in every meal

2. How many times a month do you get food from a takeaway?

a) 0–1
b) 2–3
c) 4–5
d) 6+

3. On average, how much food from your fridge gets thrown away each week?

a) We use and compost everything
b) A few leftovers that get forgotten about
c) About a quarter of what we buy
d) More than a quarter of what we buy

4. What mode of transport do you use to get to school?

a) Walk or cycle
b) Public transport (e.g. bus, train)
c) School minibus
d) Car

5. On average, how many round trips do you take by aeroplane every year?

a) None
b) One short-haul flight
c) One long-haul flight
d) More than one of either

6. Do you turn off your lights when you leave the room?

a) Yes
b) When I remember
c) I think my parents do it
d) Never

7. Do you turn off TVs and computers when you're not using them (not leaving them on standby)?

a) Yes
b) I turn the TV off but leave other things on
c) I think my parents do it
d) Never

8. Do you turn the tap off when you brush your teeth?

a) Yes
b) Most of the time, but I sometimes forget
c) Only when my parents tell me to
d) No

9. What do you do with old toys?

a) Take them to a charity shop or plan a swap shop with friends
b) Keep them – I might play with them once or twice a year
c) Leave them in a cupboard and forget about them
d) Put them in the bin

10. Which of these types of waste do you recycle/compost?

Food   Tin cans   Glass
Paper   Plastic

a) All of them
b) 3–4
c) 1–2
d) None

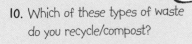

ETHICAL SHOPPING

Buying clothes and other items from a charity shop is a great way to keep stuff out of landfill. It also helps support causes in your local community.

Can you spot the following items in the charity shop on the opposite page?

Polar bear soft toy

Checked shirt

Pair of trainers

Baseball cap

Sunglasses

Backpack

Fox mug

Notebook made from recycled paper

Did You Know?

Fashion is one of the most polluting industries in the world. The next time you want to refresh your wardrobe, head to a local charity shop instead of hitting the high street. As well as supporting a good cause and keeping clothes out of landfill, you'll also be helping to slow down 'fast fashion' – clothes that are made cheaply and quickly but at a huge environmental cost.

EMISSION EQUATIONS

Complete these maths sequences to reveal how many grams of carbon are emitted by each of these modes of transport in just 1 km. Start with the number at the top and perform each sum in turn to get the final result.

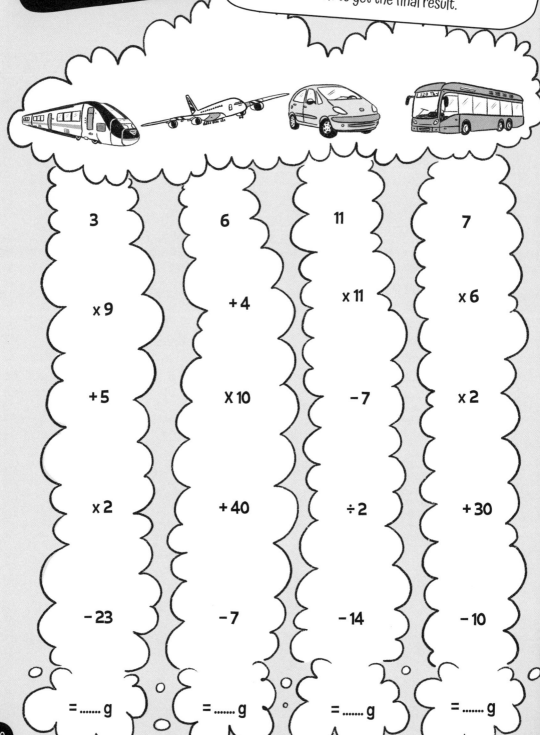

3	6	11	7
x 9	+ 4	x 11	x 6
+ 5	X 10	– 7	x 2
x 2	+ 40	÷ 2	+ 30
– 23	– 7	– 14	– 10
= .... g	= .... g	= .... g	= .... g

MEAT-FREE MEAL

Reducing the amount of meat you eat is a good way to cut down on your carbon footprint. Going totally veggie may not be for you, but eating some meat-free meals each week will make a difference to the environment.

Which set of ingredients below matches the veggie tortilla on the left exactly?

A
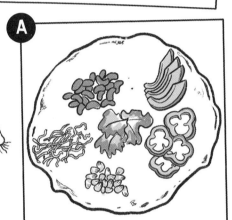

B
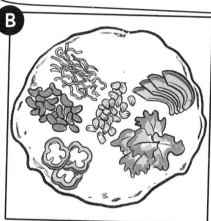

C
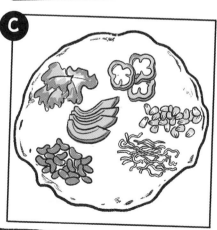

D
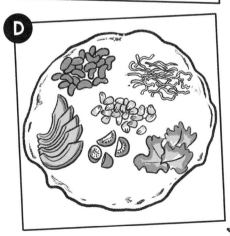

Top Tip

Many meals can be made veggie- or vegan-friendly. To encourage your family to eat less meat, suggest having one night a week where you try out new veggie recipes from around the world, such as a Mexican night with veggie tortillas like the one here.

BLEACHED BEACH

Coral can lose their colour and turn white (or 'bleach') due to changes in their environment. Can you work out which silhouette matches this piece of bleached coral exactly?

A

B

D

C

E

Did You Know?

Coral are colourful *because* of tiny algae that live inside them. When the *sea* water gets too warm, the coral become stressed, causing them to expel the algae and turn white. It is often difficult for a coral to recover from this. The main cause of coral bleaching is climate change.

REEF GRIEF

Which two tiles are not taken from this coral reef scene? And can you spot three pieces of plastic waste that shouldn't be on the reef?

A **B** **C** **D** **E** **F** **G** **H**

Top Tip

It is estimated that the equivalent of a rubbish truck full of plastic is dumped into our oceans every minute. We all need to do our bit to reduce the amount of plastic waste in the world. Say no to single-use plastics and try to use plastic-free alternatives.

SPEEDY SHOWERS

Polly is timing how long she and her family spend in the shower today, to try to cut down their water usage. She has used each person's timings to rank everyone from best (1st) to worst (5th).

Can you use the clues to work out who placed where? Who had the shortest shower and who had the longest?

- Polly didn't have the longest shower.
- Dad is four places behind Ellis.
- Natalie is two places above Dad.
- Mum is not in third place.
- Polly is above Mum.

1st place (6 mins) ....

2nd place (7 mins) ....

3rd place (9 mins) ....

4th place (11 mins) ....

5th place (15 mins) ....

Top Tip

Taking a shower instead of a bath is a really good green step ... as long as you're not spending too much time in it. You should be able to wash yourself in a shower in about 5 minutes. Encourage everyone in your household to take shorter showers to cut down on water use.

BYE-BYE, STANDBY

Ben is on a mission to turn off all the lights and appliances left on standby in his living room.

Follow the directions below to help him do this. From 'Start', follow each direction (up, down, left or right) by that number of squares. For example, U2 means you go up four squares, R4 means you go right four squares, and so on. What's the final thing that Ben turns off?

START

From the start, move D5, R2, D3, R3, U4, L3, U2, R8, D3, L2, D4, R1, U2

The final thing that Ben turns off is ....

WETLAND WONDERS

Wetlands are important habitats that are covered by water. They provide protection against flooding, purify water, store carbon and support a wide variety of animal and plant life.

Can you spot ten differences between the birds that live in this wetland scene and their reflections?

Did You Know?

A wetland can play an important role in reducing the amount of carbon that goes into the atmosphere, storing 50 times more carbon than a rainforest. Despite their importance, almost half of the world's wetlands have disappeared since 1900. Support petitions to protect wetlands and, if you live near one, pay it a visit to learn more about these incredible habitats.

SOLAR SIZES

Solar panels can come in many sizes – from portable solar panels used to charge phones to giant panels used to generate electricity for homes.

Can you work out the order of the solar panels in the field below, from biggest to smallest? Write the correct order in the space at the bottom of the page.

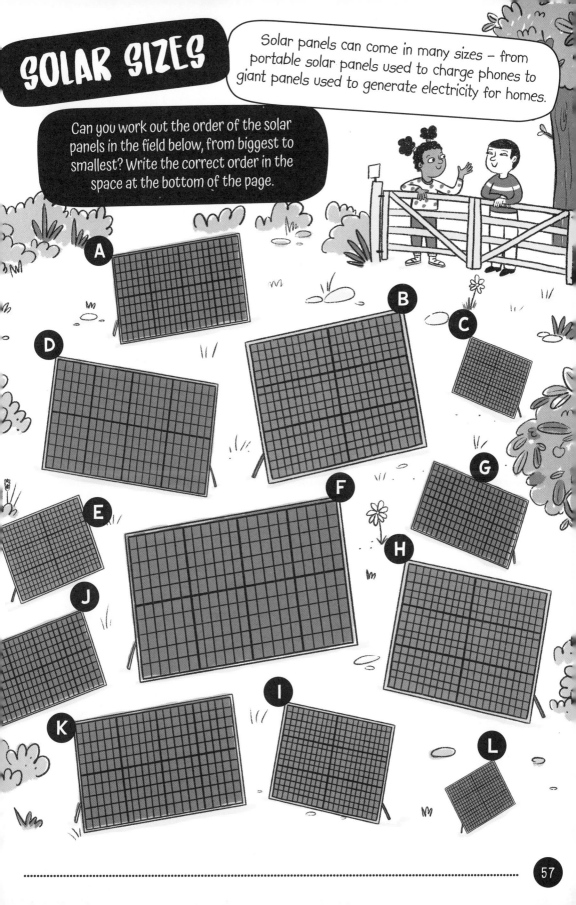

LAUNDRY DAY

Arthur wants to put on a full load of washing. To do that, he needs to find two piles of laundry whose top numbers add up to make 100.

Can you solve the number pyramids to work out the numbers at the top of each pile, then circle the two that will add together to make a full load?

A

10

8 5

B

18

7 9

C

15 16 5

D

19

12 10

E

21 27

13

58

BAG FOR LIFE

Personalize this reusable shopping bag with your own design.

Top Tip

Store your reusable shopping bags by the front door or, if you need to use a car to go to the shops, encourage your parents to keep a couple of bags in the boot. That way, you'll always have a bag to hand when you need it.

HELP FOR HEDGEROWS

Can you rearrange the panels of this picture, so they form a single scene of a hedgerow? Write the correct order from left to right underneath. The first panel is in the correct position to help get you started.

1 2 3 4 5 6 7 8 9 10

(1) ( ) ( ) ( ) ( ) ( ) ( ) ( ) ( ) ( )

Did You Know?

Hedgerows provide an important habitat for animals and plants, and also help prevent soil erosion by acting as a natural barrier between fields. But many of Europe's hedgerows have been cleared in the last century – in the UK, 50% of hedgerows have been cleared to make more space for farming.

CLIMATE CHANGE

This picture shows a glacier in Peru ten years ago.

Study the scene carefully and then see if you can spot the differences and answer the questions when you turn the page.

This picture shows what the glacier looks like today. The climate has got warmer, causing the glacier to shrink.

1. The glacier has shrunk quite a lot. Can you mark in the picture below where the glacier ended before?

2. Which mountains had snow on them in the previous picture?

3. Can you circle six other things that have changed?

PLANE SHAME

Which of the jigsaw pieces below matches one of the pieces in the main jigsaw exactly?

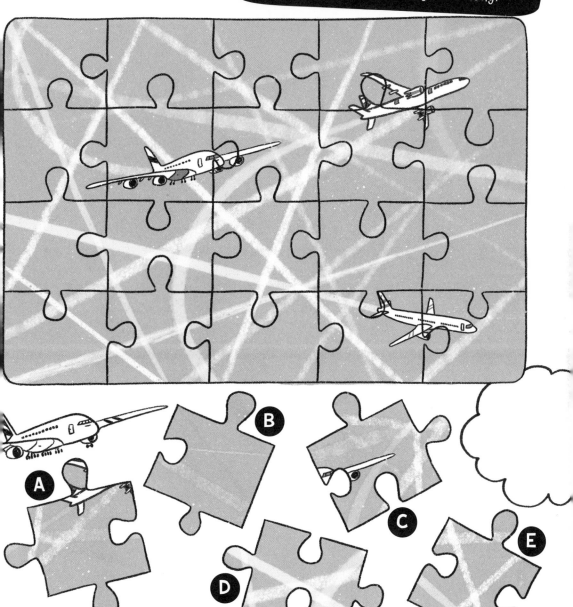

Did You Know?

A study in 2011 suggested that the white cloud trails left by planes (known as 'contrails') contribute more to global warming than all the CO_2 ever produced by aeroplanes. They are formed when water vapour freezes around soot from the plane's exhaust. Ice crystals inside these clouds trap heat and warm the climate.

FOSSIL-FUEL FACTS

Fossil fuels – such as coal, gas and oil – are the world's main source of energy. But they release carbon dioxide and other harmful greenhouse gases when they are burned, making them key contributors to global warming and climate change.

Solve the sums to learn some facts about fossil fuels. Start with the number at the top and perform each sum in turn to get the final result.

C

5
+ 8
× 6
− 34
=

Carbon dioxide produced by burning coal accounts for this percentage of global carbon emissions

A

6
× 4
+ 16
× 2
=

The percentage of the world's energy that comes from burning fossil fuels

B

10
× 20
+ 50
− 9
=

The number of coal power stations in the USA in 2019

D

12
× 12
÷ 2
+ 28
=

The number in millions of crude oil barrels used in the world per day

TURBINE TEST

Each of these houses has its own wind turbine in a square directly next to it.

Can you find all the hidden turbines in the grid by using the example and clues below? One turbine has been found for you to get you started.

Clues:

· A wind turbine is always above, below or to the side of its house – it is never diagonally next to a house.

· No wind turbine is in a square next to another wind turbine.

· The numbers around the edge of the grid tell you how many wind turbines are found in each row or column.

Example:

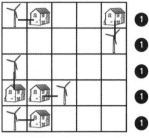

SEW CLUB

Clara and Emilio have set up a sewing club together to patch up their friends' and families' ripped or torn clothes. On average, it takes them 20 minutes to repair two rips between them.

Count all the rips in the picture below and then work out how long will it take Clara and Emilio to sew them all up.

Top Tip

Mending clothes that are slightly ripped or fixing broken items is a great way to keep things out of landfill. If you know an adult handyperson who's skilled at fixing certain things, you could ask them to show you how. Then you could set up a sewing or repair club of your own.

FARMERS' MARKET

Ella is visiting her local farmers' market.

Follow the directions to help her find her way around. From 'Start', follow each direction (up, down, left or right) by that number of squares. For example, U2 means you go up four squares, R4 means you go right four squares, and so on. Which stall does Ella end up at?

START

From the start, move D2, R7, D1, R2, D6, L4, U3, R2, D5, L7, U6, R2, U2

The stall Ella ends up at is the ....

WATER POWER

The maze below shows the inside of a hydroelectric dam. Which route does the water need to flow through to reach the generator and get out on the other side of the dam?

START

Generator

FINISH

FUN GUYS

One teaspoon of soil contains more living organisms – including bacteria, fungi and other creatures – than there are people in the world!

Can you pick out the following groups from the fungi and bugs living in this patch of earth?

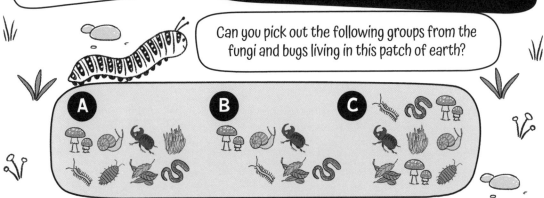

A B C

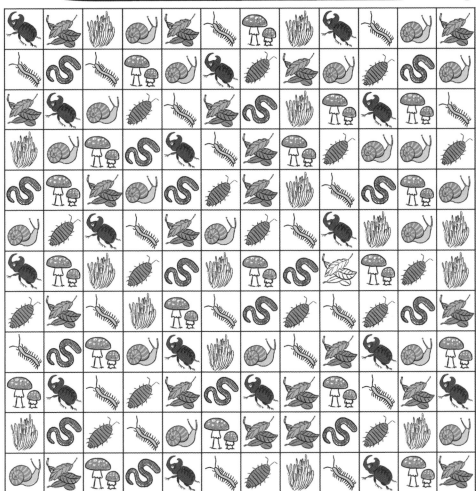

Did You Know?

Although they are small, minibeasts are vital to all life on Earth. As well as providing food for other animals and pollinating plants, many creepy crawlies also eat decaying plant matter, helping to keep the soil healthy.

SUMATRA SEARCH

How many individuals from the following groups of animals can you spot in the Sumatran scene on the opposite page?

Don't worry if you aren't sure which group they belong to – if you turn to the answer on page 95, they are listed there in detail.

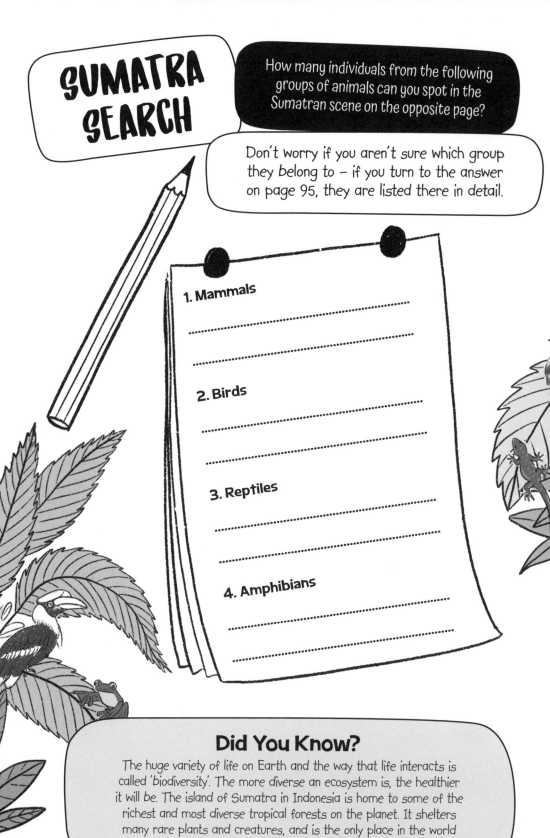

1. Mammals

....

....

2. Birds

....

....

3. Reptiles

....

....

4. Amphibians

....

....

Did You Know?

The huge variety of life on Earth and the way that life interacts is called 'biodiversity'. The more diverse an ecosystem is, the healthier it will be. The island of Sumatra in Indonesia is home to some of the richest and most diverse tropical forests on the planet. It shelters many rare plants and creatures, and is the only place in the world where tigers, rhinos, orangutans and elephants live together.

HOPPY HOMES

Can you complete the puzzle below by drawing lines to represent paths taken by frogs from one pond to another? You can only draw horizontal and vertical paths and each pond must have the same number of paths connecting it as the number printed inside it. Paths cannot cross over one another, and there can be no more than two paths joining a pair of ponds. Some paths have been added already to show you how it works.

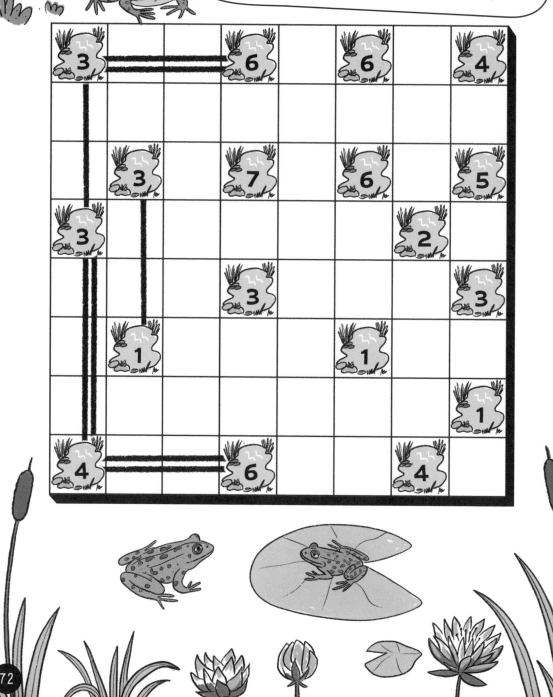

DROUGHT DISASTER

Can you help the kangaroo find a safe path to get to the pool of water? The kangaroo can only jump on patches of earth which contain a total that's a multiple of 7.

START

6 + 8

15 – 7

9 – 1

3 + 2

20 + 11

30 – 9

11 + 25

10 + 22

64 – 9

51 + 5

4 x 3

82 – 19

5 x 5

40 + 30

5 + 2

9 x 4

22 – 1

4 + 5

20 + 8

36 + 14

17 + 5

50 – 43

FINISH

Did You Know?

Between September 2019 and March 2020, Australia experienced devastating bushfires. Over 170,000 square kilometres of land was burned, and conservationists estimate that over one billion animals were killed as a result. Scientists have concluded that climate change increases the risk of such deadly fires by 30%.

DIY BIRD FEEDER

Follow these steps to make a fruity feeder for your feathered friends.

You will need:

- An apple
- Two pieces of string
- Seeds, such as sunflower or nyjer seeds
- Two thin twigs
- An apple corer

Step 1:
Ask an adult to core the apple for you.

Step 2:
Make an 'x' shape with the two twigs. Tie them together with the first piece of string.

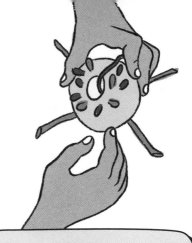

Step 3:
Place the apple on top of the 'x' and thread the second piece of string through the apple. Tie the string around the 'x' of twigs securely.

Step 4:
Push the seeds (pointy end first) gently into the skin of the apple for the birds to eat.

Step 5:
Hang your bird feeder from a tree or balcony.

Step 6:
Watch the birds enjoy their tasty snack.

Top Tip
Why not make a list of all the birds that visit the feeder and see how many different species live near you?

TURTLE COUNT

Jenna is a conservationist studying flatback sea turtles in Australia. Several months ago, three female turtles laid their eggs in underground nests on this beach. They each laid 48 eggs.

By counting the baby turtles who have just hatched in the picture, can you help Jenna work out how many eggs haven't hatched yet?

WHAT A WASTE

Fill in the number pyramid on this pile of landfill waste to discover how many years it can take a plastic toothbrush to decompose. To fill in the numbers, you need to add together the two numbers that are side by side and write the answer in the rubbish bag above them. Some numbers have been filled in already to get you started.

.... years

76

24

159   39   17   3

TOOTHBRUSH TANGLE

How many bamboo toothbrushes can you count in this jumble? And can you spot one plastic toothbrush hiding among them?

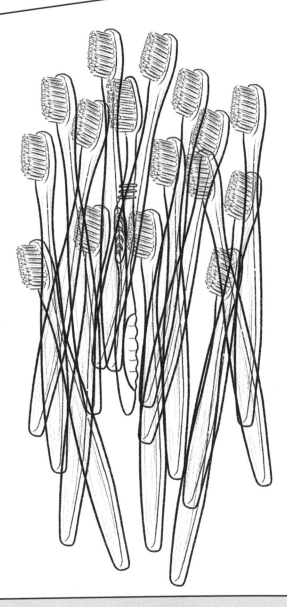

Top Tip

Consider swapping your plastic toothbrush for a bamboo brush. Unlike plastic, bamboo is a natural, biodegradable material. If you remove the bristles from the brush, you can pop the handle in the compost when it has worn out.

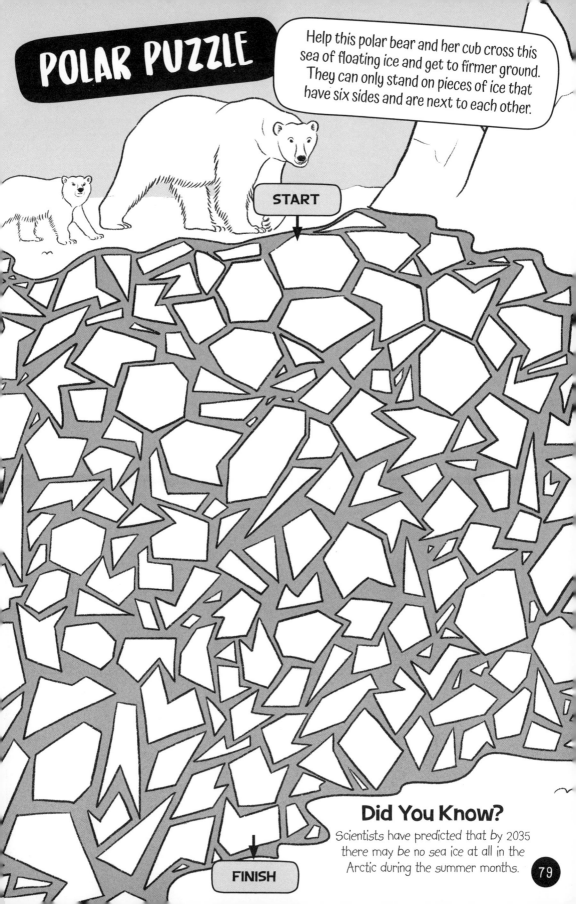

LOTS OF LAYERS

Lottie, Jackson and Raj have taken the '2-degree' challenge to cut down on their energy usage at home. They are going to wear jumpers rather than put the heating on. Each child's jumper has a different pattern on it – one has a tree pattern, one has a star pattern and one has a bird pattern. Their jumpers are also different colours – one is green, one is orange and one is blue.

By reading the following clues, can you work out which jumper belongs to which child? Once you've got the answer, draw a line to connect each child to their jumper and colour the jumpers the correct colour.

Lottie **Jackson** **Raj**

- The green jumper has stars on it.
- Jackson's jumper is blue.
- Raj's jumper has birds on it.

TRAIN TIMES

The Carter family are getting ready for their summer holiday. They have decided to travel by train rather than car to get to their campsite, to make their trip more eco-friendly.

By adding up the numbers on the four train routes, can you work out which route has the lowest total and is the quickest?

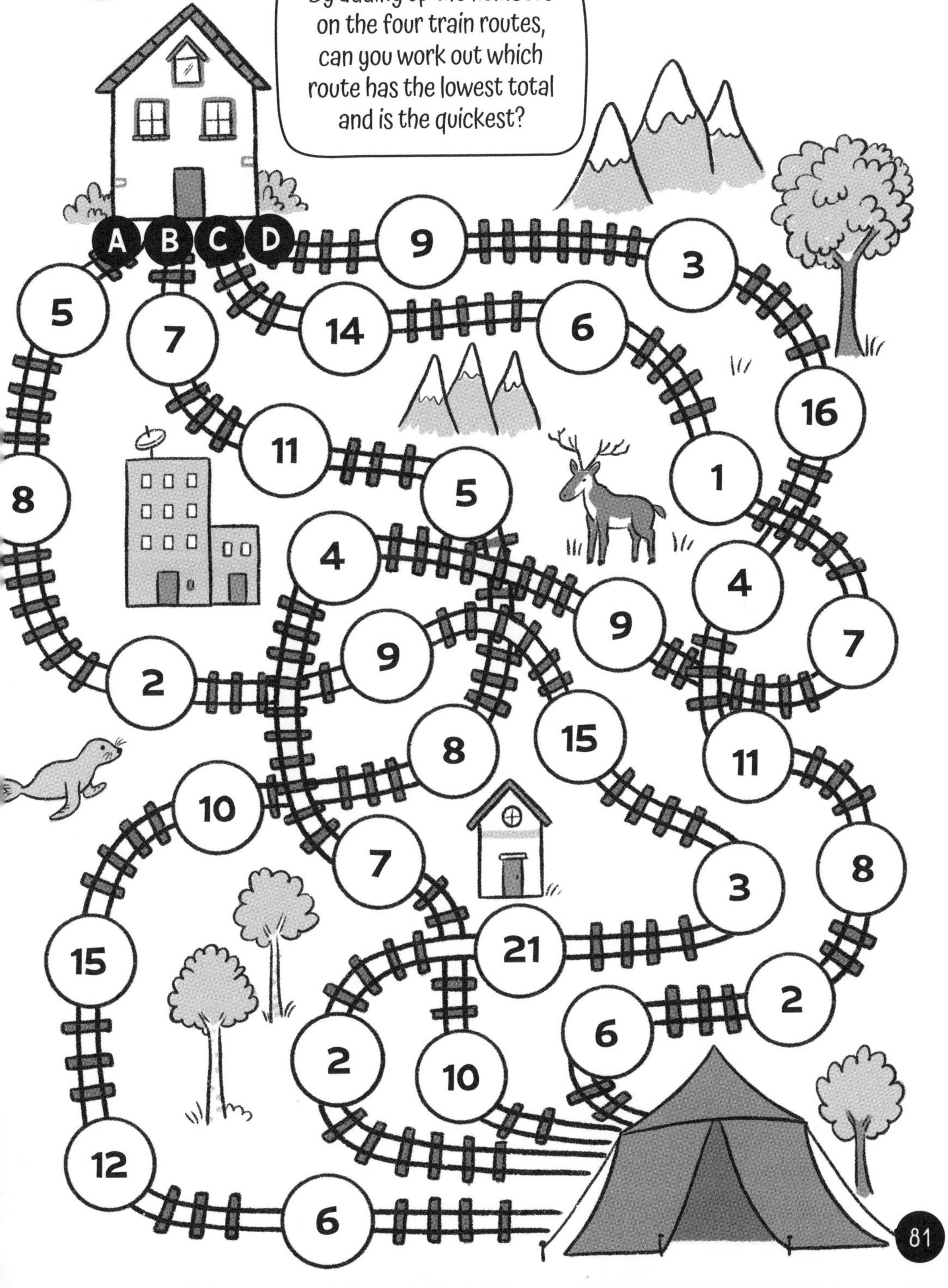

A B C D

5 7 9 3

14 6 16

8 11 5 1

4 9 4 7

2 9 8 15 11

10 7 3 8

15 21 2

2 10 6

12 6

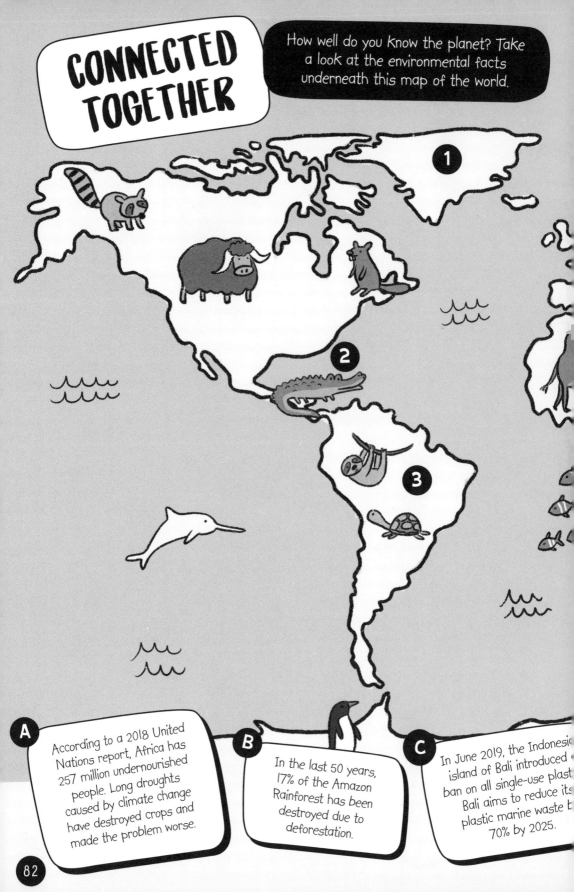

CONNECTED TOGETHER

How well do you know the planet? Take a look at the environmental facts underneath this map of the world.

A According to a 2018 United Nations report, Africa has 257 million undernourished people. Long droughts caused by climate change have destroyed crops and made the problem worse.

B In the last 50 years, 17% of the Amazon Rainforest has been destroyed due to deforestation.

C In June 2019, the Indonesia island of Bali introduced ban on all single-use plast Bali aims to reduce its plastic marine waste b 70% by 2025.

Can you match the facts to the part of the map that they refer to?

D The largest wind turbine farm in the world is being built in the Gansu province of China. When complete, it will be able to generate 20 gigawatts of energy.

E Research from NASA shows that between 1993 and 2016, Greenland lost 259 billion tonnes of ice per year.

F In 2001, there were fewer than 30 blue iguanas left in the wild. Thanks to conservationists, there are now 1,000 living wild on the Cayman Islands.

PLASTIC FREE

How many items contained in plastic packaging can you count in this shopping basket? And how many items that are loose or contained in a material that's not plastic can you spot?

If it's wrapped up in a plastic or another material, count it as one item. If the items are loose, count them individually.

Top Tip

Take your own reusable bags and containers when you go shopping to help cut down on the amount of plastic packaging you buy.

WILDLIFE-FRIENDLY FARMING

This farmer is planning his crops for the next year, and he wants to leave an area of grass in each field to grow wild, to encourage wildlife.

Can you divide the page into four separate areas using just three straight lines? Each area must contain a field, a tractor and a wildlife patch.

Did You Know?

Leaving a strip of wild plants around the edge of a crop field boosts biodiversity. It also helps to keep the farmland healthy by encouraging pollinators and insects such as ladybirds, which eat aphids and other crop pests.

STRIKE FOR THE PLANET!

Can you find the tiles at the bottom of the page within this picture of a climate march? Write your co-ordinates underneath each piece.

Top Tip

Support environmental initiatives by signing petitions or joining campaigns. Or why not organize your own? You could set up a regular 'clean-up' of your playground to make sure waste is being recycled or hold a bake sale to raise money for a conservation charity.

REBEL RULES

Use the space below to write down ten changes you want to make to help protect the planet. They could be simple goals, such as turning off the lights when you leave a room, or more long-term aims, such as taking part in a beach clean-up in the next 6 months. Whatever you choose, remember that every act – big or small – can make a real difference to the future of the environment.

ANSWERS

Page 4: River Clean-up

Page 5: Bee-utiful!
Set B contains exactly the right pieces.

Page 6: Love Your Leftovers
Here are just a few meals you could make with the ingredients - but you may have come up with many others: a salad; a cheese sandwich; a cheese and tomato sandwich; a ham sandwich; a cheese and ham sandwich; an omelette with salad; a cheese (or ham) omelette with salad; cheese on toast; pasta with tomato sauce; egg on toast; eggy bread; pasta salad; macaroni cheese.

If you thought of ten or more, you're a leftovers legend!

Page 7: Pipe Puzzle
Pipe C leads to the water butt.

Pages 8–9: Go Green
1. Solar panels – these panels create energy from the Sun's heat and don't emit any pollution.

2. Water butt – installing a water butt means you can collect rainwater to use in the garden rather than using tap water, which has been taken from rivers and other sources. This means you are reducing pressure on the environment.

3. Hanging washing outside – letting your laundry dry naturally rather than using a tumble dryer saves electricity.

4. Upcycled plant pots – this family have reused an old tyre and an old shoe to make handy plant pots. In doing so, they are keeping objects out of landfill and growing more plants, which helps keep the environment around them healthy.

5. Watering can – use a watering can to water plants rather than a garden hose, so you can keep track of how much water you are using and avoid waste.

6. Compost – composting food and garden waste reduces the amount of rubbish sent to landfill. It also turns this waste into nutrient-rich food for your garden's soil.

7. Bug hotel – a bug hotel encourages insects into your garden or outdoor space. These creatures pollinate plants and eat decaying plant matter, helping to keep your garden healthy. They are also a food source for larger animals.

8. Leave a patch of lawn unmown – this will provide a habitat for wildlife.

9. Build a pond – this will encourage wildlife in your garden, providing a home for creatures such as frogs and dragonflies.

10. Rake up leaves – raking up fallen leaves rather than using an electric blower saves unnecessary energy. Though it's also a good idea to leave a pile of leaves in your garden, to act as a cosy home for wildlife.

Page 10: Pollinator Sudoku

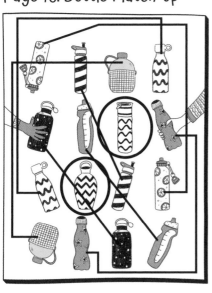

Pages 11–12: Pollinator Power

1. Apple tree
2. Ivy, chives, sedum, rosemary, lavender, dandelions, crocus and strawberry
3. A strawberry; there were 6 strawberry fruits
4. A garden rake
5. 3 bugs (worm, butterfly, bee)

Page 13: Bottle Match-up

Page 14: Dolphin Dilemma

Stream B leads to the fish.

Page 15: Orangutan Stats

a) 26 - 8 ÷ 2 - 6 = 3
b) 5 × 4 + 28.5 × 2 = 97%
c) 104 ÷ 4 - 14 ÷ 6 = 2 metres
d) 16 × 3 + 52 ÷ 2 = 50 years
e) 30 + 42 ÷ 4 - 11 = 7 years

Page 16: Quick Fix

Page 17: Running On Empty

Car C is on a road that will lead to the charging point.

Page 18: Turbine Jumble

13

Page 19: Wonder Wall

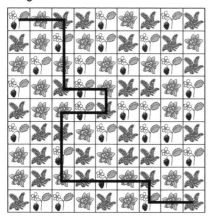

Page 21: Plastic Problem

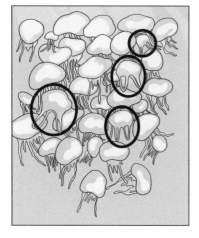

Page 24: Compost Champions

A = 38 B = 27 C = 22
Compost bin A has the best compost.

Page 25: Grow Green

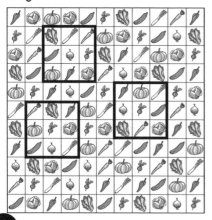

Pages 26–27: Eco Home

	MONDAY	TUESDAY	WEDNESDAY	THURSDAY	FRIDAY	SATURDAY	SUNDAY
Water the plants		Laila				Ezra	
Sort the recycling			Laila				
Empty compost bin			Ezra				
Cook a meat-free meal	Dad Laila			Mum Ezra			
Do a food shop						Mum Laila	
Do a clothes wash						Dad	
Clean the bike							Ezra

Page 28: Wonky Veg Waste

Silhouette C

Page 29: Eco Energy

A = wind power   B = solar power
C = nuclear   D = electricity

Page 30: On Your Bike!

Amira's bike is the medium-sized bike and it's called the 'Eco Warrior'. Ryan's bike is the largest bike and it's called the 'Green Goer'. Jess's bike is the smallest bike and it's called the 'Pedal Powerer'.

Page 31: Shoe Match-up

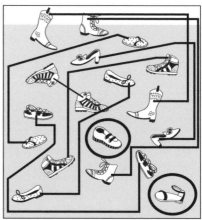

Page 32: Small Actions, Big Change

The energy saved from recycling one glass bottle will operate a 100-watt light bulb for four hours.

Making aluminium from recycled materials takes 95% less energy than using raw materials.

Turning off the tap when you brush your teeth can save over 24 litres of water a day.

Preventing one tonne of paper waste saves between 15 and 17 mature trees.

A ten-year-old TV left on standby uses 12 watts per hour.

By carrying reusable cutlery or reusing your plastic cutlery you can save 466 items of unnecessary plastic every year.

Every year, eight million tonnes of plastic waste is dumped into the ocean.

Page 33: Recycling Sudoku

Page 34: Plant Power

It will take Luca 135 minutes (or 2 hours, 15 minutes) to plant all 15 saplings in the picture. This is because 9 minutes x 15 saplings = 135 minutes.

Page 35: Tree-rific

a) $2 + 4 \times 9 - 4 \times 100 = 5{,}000$ years
b) $14 + 6 \times 5 \times 10 \times 2 = 2{,}000$ species
c) $8 \times 6 + 5 + 10 \div 3 = 21$ kilograms
d) $7 \times 3 + 4 \times 5 - 18 = 107$ metres

Page 36: Smart Thinking

Tv = 6
Smartphone = 1
Video game = 5
Toaster = 7

Page 38: Sloth Crossings

Sloth A = Tree 2
Sloth B = Tree 3
Sloth C = Tree 4
Sloth D = Tree 1

Page 39: A Load Of Rubbish

Paper and cardboard bin = 9 items
Glass, plastic and tin bin = 7 items
Food waste bin = 9 items (counting each half of egg shell as a separate item)

Pages 40–41: Leopard Trail

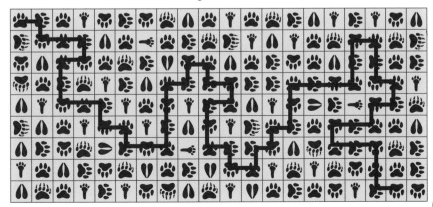

Page 42: This Old Thing

Here are some ideas for ways to reuse an old T-shirt – but you may have thought of many others: a DIY no-sew bag (see pages 22–23); tie-dye or decorate it so it looks like a new T-shirt; cut off the sleeves and turn it into a vest; cut it into strips to use as headbands or fabric bracelets; tie the strips together to make a dog tug toy; use the fabric to make pompoms; use a square of it to patch up another piece of clothing; use multiple squares to make a quilt; use the fabric to make a stuffed toy; use leftover strips to make laces.

Page 43: Lunchbox Wars

Lunchbox A = 3 points in total
Lunchbox B = 5 points in total
Lunchbox C = 1 point in total
Lunchbox B is the most eco-friendly.

Pages 46-47: How Eco-Friendly Are You?

Mostly As – You're an eco pro. You're committed to helping the planet and are always looking for ways to make your life greener. You also encourage your friends and family to do the same.

Mostly Bs – You're doing your bit to help the planet and have already made lots of changes to make your lifestyle greener. You sometimes forget to stick to these initiatives, though.

Mostly Cs – You try to do your bit but tend to rely on Mum and Dad to remind you to switch off lights and recycle. It's time to make some of these changes yourself.

Mostly Ds – You're acting like there's a Planet B! Try to introduce some changes to your lifestyle. Remember that even small things – like turning off the tap when you brush your teeth – can make a huge difference.

Pages 48-49: Ethical Shopping

Page 50: Emission Equations

Train: 3 × 9 + 5 × 2 – 23 = 41 g
Plane: 6 + 4 × 10 + 40 – 7 = 133 g
Car: 11 × 11 –7 ÷ 2 – 14 = 43 g
Bus: 7 × 6 × 2 + 30 – 10 = 104 g

Page 51: Meat-Free Meal

Tortilla C has the exact ingredients.

Page 52: Bleached Beach

Coral C

Page 53: Reef Grief

Tiles A and C don't match the main image. The three things that shouldn't be on the reef are: a plastic bag, a cotton bud and a bottle.

Page 54: Speedy Showers

1st place (6 mins) = Ellis
2nd place (7 mins) = Polly
3rd place (9 mins) = Natalie
4th place (11 mins) = Mum
5th place (15 mins) = Dad

Page 55: Bye-Bye, Standby

The final thing that Ben turns off is the smartphone (or smartphone charger).

Page 56: Wetland Wonders

Page 57: Solar Sizes

F, B, H, D, K, A, I, J, G, E, C, L

Page 58: Laundry Day

The top numbers of C and E will add together to make a full load.

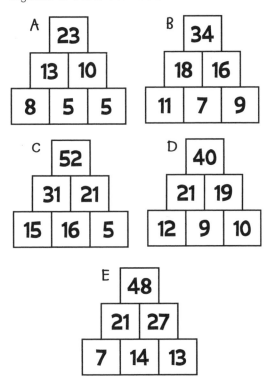

A
23	
13	10
8	5	5

B
34	
18	16
11	7	9

C
52	
31	21
15	16	5

D
40	
21	19
12	9	10

E
48	
21	27
7	14	13

Page 60: Help For Hedgerows

The correct order is: 1, 8, 7, 4, 3, 6, 2, 10, 5, 9

Pages 61–62: Climate Change

1) The glacier used to extend below the tree (circled below).

2) There was snow on two other mountains in the first picture (circled below).

3) The six other things that have changed are: There are now more fields of crops in the valley; the tree has died; the plants in the second picture are not as big as they were in the first picture; there aren't as many birds in the sky; there aren't as many clouds; there is now a lake in the valley.

Page 63: Plane Shame

Piece D

Page 64: Fossil-Fuel Facts

a) $6 \times 4 + 16 \times 2 = 80\%$
b) $10 \times 20 + 50 - 9 = 241$ stations
c) $5 + 8 \times 6 - 34 = 44\%$
d) $12 \times 12 \div 2 + 28 = 100$ million

Page 65: Turbine Test

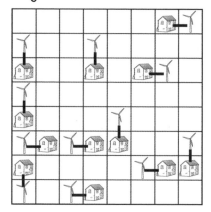

Pages 66: Sew Club

It will take Clara and Emilio 160 minutes (or 2 hours, 40 minutes) to repair all of the rips in the picture. There are 16 rips in the picture and we know that it takes Clara and Emilio 20 minutes to repair 2 rips between them. $16 \div 2 = 8$ and $8 \times 20 = 160$.

Page 67: Farmers' Market

Ila ends up at the bread stall.

Page 68: Water Power

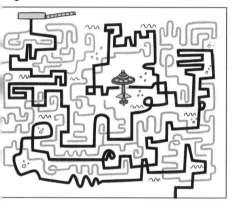

Page 69: Fun Guys

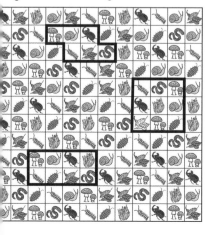

Pages 70–71: Sumatra Search

Mammals: 16 in total (3 forest elephants, 3 Sumatran rhinos, 3 Sumatran orangutans, 2 clouded leopards, 3 Sumatran tigers, 2 flying-fox bats)
Birds: 4 in total (2 kingfishers, 1 hornbill, 1 peacock pheasant)
Reptiles: 8 in total (2 geckos, 2 water monitors, 1 reticulated python, 2 Asian vine snakes, 1 false gharial – a type of crocodile)
Amphibians: 2 in total (2 Wallace's flying frogs)

Page 72: Hoppy Homes

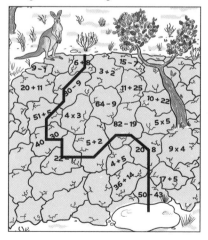

Page 73: Drought Disaster

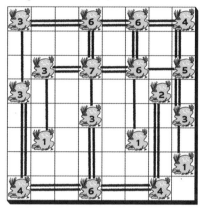

Page 76: Turtle Count

You know that 3 mother turtles each laid 48 eggs. 48 x 3 = 144. There are 33 baby turtles that have hatched in the picture. 144 - 33 = 111. So there are 111 eggs left to hatch.

Page 77: What a Waste

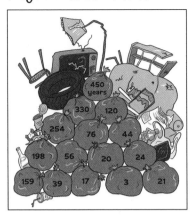

Page 78: Toothbrush Tangle

There are 15 bamboo toothbrushes.

Page 79: Polar Puzzle

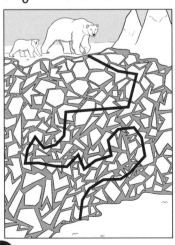

Page 80: Lots of Layers

Lottie's jumper is green and has stars on it.
Jackson's jumper is blue and has trees on it.
Raj's jumper is orange and has birds on it.

Page 81: Train Times

a) 65   b) 74
c) 58   d) 59
Route C is the fastest route.

Pages 82–83: Connected Together

A (Africa) = 4
B (Amazon Rainforest) = 3
C (Bali) = 6
D (China) = 5
E (Greenland) = 1
F (Cayman Islands) = 2

Page 84: Plastic Free

8 items use plastic packaging: 1 milk bottle,
1 juice bottle, 1 broccoli in plastic wrap, 1 pack
of tomatoes, 2 ready-meals, 1 pack of bananas,
1 pack of doughnuts.
10 items are plastic free: 1 cucumber, 3 peppers,
1 lettuce, 3 carrots, 1 leek, 1 loaf of bread in a
paper bag.

Page 85: Wildlife-Friendly Farming

Page 86: Strike for the Planet!

D7, I5, H8, A6, D4, H3, D2, F5